Timeless Souls

The Poetry of Rainey Moon

Rainey Moon Publishing
Chester, VA

Published by The Lair
Chester, VA
www.raineymoon.com

Copyright ©2004 by The Lair. All rights reserved.
All photography, artwork and poems are property of Rainey Moon Publishing. No part of this book may be reproduced or transmitted in any form or by any means without written permission from the publisher.

Publisher's Cataloging-in-Publication Data
Timeless Souls
By Rainey Moon
ISBN: 0-9747941-7-1

First Edition
Printed & Published in the United States of America
Cover & Interior Artwork by Rainey Moon

Contents

Timeless Souls	7
An Angel's Heart Cries	8
Mazes of Life	9
Darkness	10
Deep Within His Thoughts	11
Comfort My Pain	11
So I Follow	12
Wonder Why	13
A Tear Drop On The Fire	14
The Tree	15
Ghost In This House	16
Tears Falling	17
I Stay The Same	18
I am Free	19
Never Knew	20
Beautiful Angels	21
A Sweet Dream I Never Had	22
A Leaf Goes Floating By	23
Opium Dreams	24
Darkness Calls	25
Avidity	26
Ashes to Ashes	27
Incubus	28
Walkin' Along	29
I Don't Exist	30
Blossom of The Sun's Love	31
The Odyssey	33
Damn! It's Good To Be Back To Me	34
A Raven Called Out On The Wind	35
Rapture	37
Lost To The Sadness This Heart Beats Of	38
Temptations of Imagination	39
Not Yet	40
I Called To You	41
Our World of Immortality	42
Winter's Rain	43
Enraptured	44
Days of Old	45
Lost To This Hell In Me	46
In The Shadows of a Falling Moon	47
Felt You There	48
A Gypsy Soul	49
A Darkness Reigns	50
A Spirit With No Place To Go	51
A Long Day's Pains	52

Contents

Needing You	53
The Storm	54
Touching You	55
I Die	56
Scream At Me	57
An Angel	58
A Lullaby	59
The Loneliness of My Soul	60
Eternal Damnation	61
Sweet Imaginations	62
My Nirvana	63
The Angel of Death	64
Mad Woman In The Graveyard Growing Old	65
Two Lovers Dance	66
So Tired of Being Here	67
Building Anticipation	68
Days In The Shadows	69
Voices	70
Still of Night	71
Have You Seen His Beauty?	72
This Cold In Me	73
Reflection	74
Rest In Peace	75
Can't Help I'm Not The Same	76
Eyes of Ecstasy	77
A Canvas of White	78
Fallen Sunsets	79
You Can Never Go	80
Whispers Of The Soul Emit	81
The Forest	82
Two Lost Souls	83
The Ghost's Tale	86
Left Behind	88
Dawn Fades To Night	88
Befallen	89
A Blanket For Scars	90
My Time to Fly	90
Letting Go	91
Long Lost Mind	92
A Piano Plays Softly	93
Eyes Closed	93
Lover's Drum	94
Here With You	94

Timeless Souls

Do you hear
The angels calling
As their hearts
Are Falling
Do you feel
The north wind blowing
As their souls
Continue going
In a downward spiral
Into the misty fog
Scared - alone
Knowing their wrongs
Never a chance
To be righted
Never a chance
To be flighted
With the wings
Of the children
Of the lamb
No one can save them
No one can
Timeless souls
Lost to the wind
Adrift in darkness
So lost within
Do you hear
The angels calling
As they go gently
Softly falling

Fallen Angels
From Above
Lost to the heavens
Lost from love
Beautiful angels
Drifting near
Beautiful voices
Sweet and clear
Timeless souls
Lost to the wind
Adrift in spirit
Not knowing
Where to begin
Voices calling
Angels falling
Reaching out to you
For a moments touch
Not asking or taking
Too much
Just looking for
A warm embrace
As they fall
From God's Grace
Tear stained eyes
Hearts that weep
Wishing - only wishing
Their soul he would keep

An Angels Heart Cries

There's a tear fallen from the sky
An angel lost to darkness
An angel's heart that cries
Saddened so upon the earth
Death became her wish
To fly with the angels
To be lifted to the mists
Her heart breaking
Her soul aching
She took her life away
Because with the angels
Was where she wished
To spend her days
She felt the blade
She watched the blood fall
She rose from her body
She heard the angels call
Up she went to the heavens above
To find her rescue in God's love
Beautiful angels filled with life
Flowed around her there
Her heart weightless without care
Finally her pain would go
Finally happiness she would know
The closer she came
The more strange
Everything seemed to be
Beautiful angels with tear stained eyes
Held her close and began to cry
She felt her happiness grow to fear
The closer they drew her near

One angel whispered then
"He will not let you in,
For in your life you did sin"
Oh how her heart was breaking
Oh how her soul was aching
Wrapped there in the love of angels
She found she was not able
To remain there in their love
To stay in the heavens above
They kissed her softly upon her brow
And cast her falling, falling down
There's a tear fallen from the sky
An angel lost to darkness
An angel's heart that cries

Mazes of Life Through The Trees

Leaves are falling
To the ground
Stripping the forest
Into its' nakedness
Looking carefully
You can see
The mazes of life
Through the trees

Slowly the snow
Begins to fall
Gently lying against
The forest wall
Sunshine blinding your eyes
You cannot see
The mazes of life
Through the trees

Spring has come
With it's vigor and love
The birds are chirping nearby
Nesting as high
As the sky
The forest has become green
Lost are the mazes of life
Through the trees

Walking into the forest
It becomes
Each maze
Turning into one
Which way is out?
How do you find your way
Searching further
Into your dismay
You search frantically
Night and day
In the mazes of life
Through the trees

Darkness

A darkness calling to me
Alluring, desiring, beckoning
Wanting me to embrace
To fall from grace
To feel pleasures concealed
In the crevices of its appeal
Fascination, intrigue overcome
Watching myself as I come undone
Giving into the temptation
Walking into without hesitation
A deadly embrace of lure
For which there is no cure
A dance for the erotic
A slumber for the exotic
Yearning for, entangled in thee
Adrift upon his magical seas
Lost to the abyss of desire
Burning quenching fires
Pleasures soon to be revealed
Wandering through your fields
Of delightful play
Darkness beckons, I stay
Within a newfound realm of beauty
Ahh tis my soul's duty
Floating aloft inside of you
Darkness awakened calling unto
Wanting me for lustrous tumble
Yearnings inside rumble
Forth from a long nights rest
Putting my heart to the test
The darkness has overcome
That to which I now am one
Embraced by its divine lure
For which I want no cure.
Rescued from the light
As darkness becomes my life

Deep Within His Thoughts

A soul of the truest heart
So deep within his thoughts
I wonder what he thinks
As I watch him float away
I know there is beauty there
Of what I cannot know
Feeling it emit from all around
Flowing from him to me
As he drifts to wander
Deep within his thoughts
Wishing I could be there
To be so close
To touch the beauty
That gently floats
From him to me
As I watch him falling
Into a thoughtful sea

Comfort My Pain

Tumbling Tumbling
Through the abyss
Never returning
Set adrift
Upon a sea of tears
Heart stolen
Soul fallen
Never to feel
Another emotion
Pain my comfort
Comfort my pain
Reverse the change

Take hold of me
Catch me before I fall
Be the voice I can hear
Help me return
Don't let my soul burn
Wrap me in wings divine
So that I may climb
Into the womb of mercy
Cleanse my soul
Make me whole
So that I no longer decend
Here among the fallen

So I Follow

My heart is breaking
I have fell in love
I know not his name
I have seen him but once
A heart of gold
A soul of laughter
Happiness beams
All around him
Colors emit
An aura of beauty
Magical essence
I cannot catch
I follow
Closely behind
If only to grab a glimpse
Of the angel
That dances before me
My heart weeps
Because I know
There before me
Is a free soul
Never to be mine
Never in time
So I follow
Closely
If only to catch
A glimpse
Of the beauty
His soul emits

Wonder Why

I danced there under the moon
Happy to know no more
Would I feel the pain
Lost to the night, no longer day
Laid me to rest today

Spirit rose, up I danced
Songs about, heart free
Saw the mourners here
Earlier today when
They covered my body

Tears shed, hearts sad
Guess its just too bad
Didn't seem to matter then
Didn't seem to matter when
I was still alive

Just a shadow in their life
An acquaintance, a passerby
Now I am the reason they all cry
Wonder why
As I dance here under the moon

Spirit lifted hearts gloom
No longer my burden to bear
No more pain no more cares
The moon my lover
The stars my light

Soul adrift, spirit in flight
There I danced all throughout the night
Watching over those I loved
Wonder why
I'm the reason they all cry

A Tear Drop On The Fire

A tear drop on the fire
Bursting into flames
Feel my hunger
Feel my pain
Searching for escape
Falling from grace
Knowing my end is near
Seeing ever clear
The visions of death
That beckon my soul
Desiring my spirit
I can't let go
Not ready to leave
Not willing to follow
Into the darkness
So cold, so hollow
How will I find
The release I need
I beg, I cry, I plead
Tears are falling
The darkness calling
Away I pull from its grasp
My heart bleeding
My soul collapsed
Never giving up the fight
Never surrendering to the night
Take my pain
Take my hunger
Take my soul
As I go under
Leaving only one remain
A tear drop in the flame
An eternal vigil to my fight
My stand against the night

The Tree

Tears washed down her face
As she stared out through the rain
Her heart breaking love lost today
Hearing the wheels screaming
Across the pavement to the tree
That took away her happiness
And dreams of yesterday
Waiting for him to come home
Knowing he never would again
Because today her true love
Fell into eternal sleep
Lost so far away in his dreams
Where she only wished she could be
Her hand she pressed against the glass
As if reaching for one last touch
Her heart lost to sadness
Oh she loved him so much
To scared to walk away
If for just one moment
He could be there alone
And she miss him
Just when he needed to say
Goodbye my darling
In my heart you'll always stay

Ghost In This Home

I'm just a ghost in this home
Lost to the sadness of being alone
Shattered by the loss of you
Red eyes once blue
Sleep never comes
Not even once
Walls echo, walls scream
Nights lost without a dream

I'm just a ghost in this home
Lost to the sadness of being alone
Shadow of a soul
That cannot let go
Of the man who used to live here too
Of the love once true
You're no longer here
All that's left of me is tears

I'm just a ghost in this home
Lost to the sadness of being alone
All that's left of two hearts in love
Lost somewhere in the mist above
Shadow of a soul
That cannot let go
I'm just a ghost in this home

Tears Falling

Tears falling can't catch them now
Don't want to, don't know how
Have to release this pain in me
Have to find a release
Before I fall completely apart
Lost somewhere here in the dark
Forever dying from the sadness within
Never knowing how to begin
To pick up the pieces and move on
To right the things that went wrong
I scream out into the night
Tears falling blinding my sight
Have to let this all go
Never felt so alone
Never felt so lost and afraid
Don't know how I face each day
I somehow get up and be
Not knowing this person not knowing me
Tears falling can't catch them now
Don't want to don't know how
Lost somewhere here in the darkness
That has become my home
Heart breaks so alone
Soul lost to the tears that fall away
Tears falling but the loneliness stays
I scream out into the night
Filled with sadness, lost sight
Of a day where the light shines in
Of a day when I can love again
Tears falling can't catch them now
Don't want to, don't know how

I Stay The Same

As I drift quietly to sleep
I see your tears and hear you weep
Not knowing why you cry
Not understanding why
As others gather closer in
I see the pain again
Sadness overwhelms their soul
For why I do not know
I reach for them to ease their pain
But nothing moves I stay the same
Sleep fills me yet I'm so afraid
To close my eyes today
I begin to see what has become of me
Through the tears of thee
Images dance in the streams
Of a person I have never seen
Lying there in the shadows of your tears
Aged over a hundred years
I reach for you to rescue me
To awaken me from this dream
I want to hold you close again
I don't want this to end
I reach for you to ease my pain
But nothing moves I stay the same

I Am Free

Drunken by a midnight sun
Floating about here among
The tall dark trees
That stand strong against the sky
The moon's light blinding my eyes
I am free

Stars aloft in the clear skies
A raven calls and echoes
Through the core of my soul
My heart adrift my spirit soars
I feel pain no more
I am free

I take my flight to the ground
I wrap myself in nights' shroud
Protecting me from what once was
Admiring the beauty of who I have become
Leaves rustle through the trees
I am free

Behind a shadow I now stand
Alone but no longer sad
I took my flight away from life
I became a raven upon the night
I come and go as I please
I am free

Sorrows lost to reality
Death became me
Lost now in a dream
Hollowed heart alive again
Softly in joy it beats
I am free

Life once loved, death feared
I found my solace here
Among the shadows in the grove
Free my spirit roams
No more sadness no more pain
I am free

Never Knew

Blue skies fading to gray
Feelin the wind pullin me away
Falling back into a midnight whirl
Knowing I am leaving this world
Catch me catch me if you can
If I had a chance would have ran
Don't wanna fall to the black
Wanna another chance gotta come back

Lost now to my dying wish
Felt the blade enter
Watched the blood spill
Cried from the wounds revealed
Yes it all just went away
Drifted through and out my mind
No one came to rescue me
From this misery

Take it all back if only I could
If I could take it all back I would
Never knew it would hurt like this
Now I lay here in this dark abyss
Wishing I could hold you one more time
Only I am gone now to far from touch
Never knew I would miss you this much

Beautiful Angels

Beautiful Angels
Drifting about
I wonder
Where I am
Not understanding
Is it a dream
Or have I passed
Through the gates
That guard the darkness

Have I left this place
That I have come to know
Have I lost my way
To come back home
Tell me this is but
A dream I am lost within
Please don't tell me
I have left you
Never to return

How will I remain here
With the angels above
How will I go on
Without your love?
I do not wish to be
A shadow in the dark
I want to return
Away from this place
That forever will entrap me
Confining me
From your touch

You the angel
I need so
You the lover
True loves know
I need to stay here with you
I cannot go across
To the other side
I cannot live here
In the dark

Beautiful Angels
Drifting about
I wonder
Where I am
Not understanding
Is it a dream
Or have I passed
Through the gates
That guard the darkness

A Sweet Dream I Never Had

A beautiful sunrise
I wanted to share
Wanted you
To be there
You chose another path
Aside my heart was cast
In sadness I sit here alone
Wishin I would have known

You're a spirit I cannot capture
You're the reason for my rapture
A sweet dream I never had
The one who causes me to hurt so bad

Waited for you time and again
Thinkin maybe you would begin
To feel this love I have for you
To know how true
Love could be
If you could only see
Wishin I would have known

You're a spirit I cannot capture
You're the reason for my rapture
A sweet dream I never had
The one who causes me to hurt so bad

Feel like a kid again
Trying to catch night bugs
Knowing no matter how well it goes
Should I place you in my jar
You would be dead by tomorrow
A spirit killed by capture
The reason for my rapture
A sweet dream I never had
The one I want so bad

A Leaf Goes Floating

By

As a leaf goes floating by
Under the tree where I rest
Lying upon my back looking up
Searching for whatever may be
Existing there in the world above
I wonder

Hues of green brown and gold
All combined becoming whole
Though falling apart it stands
In majesty against all odds
Rays of light shimmer in
Bits of blue emit
Just like me

Leaves falling, leaves clinging on
Branches supporting holding strong
Winter will soon be upon this mighty spirit
Striping it of its beauty
But forever it stands on
Waiting for the spring sun
To rejuvenate to refill
It's Soul

I wonder does it fear
That the new sun won't come
That the winter will live on
Forever in its soul
Wanting to hold on to what remains
For fear it won't come back again.

Does its heart ache with each fallen leaf
Knowing soon it will be barren an unshielded
For what lay in wait
For what could come
Or for what may be the end
Of its very existence
Just like me

Maybe it has a shimmer of hope
That blue skies will return
That Orange Brown and Green
Will combine becoming one
Beautiful color for the world to see
Maybe the winter's cold
Will be kind to its soul

Opium Dreams

Chased the Dragon
Caught the Moon
Smoke hazed room
The images dance
Feeling quite high
Left in a trance
Gave in to the pain
That called my name
Drifted to darkness
Opium Dreams

Felt ecstasy
So close yet so far
Touched by a phantom
Kissed by death
Lost in a world
So peaceful to me
Numb to the sorrows
Awake yet sleeping
Opium Dreams

Eyes closed
To the sadness around
Nothing but existence
Enraptures me now
Feel your touch
But you're so far away
Lost to the abyss
Of a dream gone bad
Drifting further away
Soon I will be free
Freed from my Opium dreams

Darkness Calls

Darkness looms
I hear it calling
Reaching out to me
From the depths of night
I take my leave
I take flight
To fall with the angels below
Knowing this the destiny
Of my long lost soul
Voices singing
Bodies clinging
Holding on to all that's left
As we drift further
Into the abyss
Peace of mind
Lost to time
I the fallen angel
That carries on
Dreams aflight
Dreams of night
Darkness calls
I answer with my cries
As I spread my wings
I fly

Avidity

Consumed with avidity
Lost in a dream
Drifting in and out of thought
Thoughts of you and me

Imagining our bodies
Making love
My lips water
My eyes close
Needing you so

What have I become
Body aching
For your touch
Nothing stopping
Devoured by you

A demon that dances
Behind the shadows of lust
Bringing me to this
Loss of innocence
So intense

My hands touch
To heal the pain
Of the hunger
From which I crave
Disgrace?

Cannot care
I crave too much
Need to imagine
Your touch
I touch

Body heated
By images of you
Imaginations of your touch
Become my own
I succumb

Fall to the pleasures
That you would give
Believing them my own
Were you here
Wetness comes

Body supple
Breast erect
My gardens so wet
I come unto
Imaginations of you

Heart spent
Body weak
I fall into sleep
Dreams of you
Refresh anew
This burning

Burning of avidity
Lost in a dream
Drifting in and out of thought
Thoughts of you and me

Ashes To Ashes

Ashes to ashes
Dust to Dust
Sinful play
Turns to lust
Wanting you
Needing your touch
Bodies wet
Eyes a gaze
Beauty betwixt
The sheets of haze.

Powerful surges
Deeper still
Lost to ecstasy
Getting my fill
Tasting your soul
Drinking your blood
Lost in the power
Of delightful love

My body atop
My body beneath
Come from behind
And make me scream
Needing you
Wanting you more
Falling faster
Faster still
Screaming your name
Robbed of my will

Delightful yearnings
Turned to lust
Ashes to ashes
Dust to dust

Incubus

Just as darkness settles on the land
My body awakens to the sounds of night
Lifted by its spirit that drifts about so clear
Knowing my time is near
Lights are illuminating the western sky
Peace has come and I rise
Searching for the incubus of my days
For at rest he lays
Lost to a world of dreams
While I come searching for him
Walking in the shadows of his night
To touch his soul as he has mine
Only darkness doesn't last not enough time
To engulf him wholly into my world
Lost to a sunrise, his body begins to whirl
Awakening to know his dreams of me
Remembering the journey through ecstasy
The ride he has rode time again
Aching to know who I am
A vision of beauty in his eyes
Lost to the succubus who resides
Deep in his nights of sleep
The one who makes his soul weep
Every morning when the sun begins to rise
Knowing no more than the night before
Feeling the hunger creeping in
Lost to her touch through the day
As slowly I lay down to rest
Knowing his thoughts my dreams will possess

Walkin' Along

There I was
Walkin' along
Humming. Humming
Humming my song
Sky was gray
The wind
From the west
I walked
Walked along

Kicked a can
Threw a rock
Thinking bout
All my
Private thoughts
Thoughts of you
Thoughts of me
Lost to this
Song in me

On I walked
Humming my song
While I went along
Sadness wore
Upon my soles
Of times with you
But in the music
Of it all
I walked along
Humming my song

Thought of
That time when
We were just
Hanging out
There on the shore
Drawing pictures
In the sand
Laughing, talking
Holding hands

A smile
Upon my face
Even though
Your gone
Of happy times
A thought embraced
Humming our song
As I walked
Walked along

I Don't Exist

Delightful play
Lost to a haze
Feel myself lifted
Away from here
Euphoria my realm
Non existent
Here but unaware
Floating adrift
Through my mind
Which has no meaning
I don't exist
Feel the pleasures
Of my heart beating
Knowing I am breathing
Knowing I am alive
Dead to the outside
Awake in consciousness
Ready to fly
Grounded to reality
Fighting nothing
I don't exist
Body tingles
Mind wavers
In a trance
Lost to the dance
Existing in me
Warm and Alive
Cannot see
The world outside
Intoxicated
Ecstasy

Blossom of the Sun's Love

A blossom from
The morning sun
Ready to face the world
She took upon
Her young heart
A beau to call her own
Young and free
Beautiful and naive
She let her heart give way
She fell in love to stay
Her first love so dear
Her heart so clear
Nothing their to guide
Herself through the nigh
She let the emotions swim
She let them begin
To grow to such
An ecstatic state
Her first hearts dance
Swept away in its trance

Lost her to this young beau
The daughter of the sun
Who blossomed and became
No longer a girl that day
She let go
And let her grow
Knowing what pain
Would come to pass
Oh how her heart did hurt
As she let her blossom grow
Into a woman of love's woe

For many a day
The blossom played
There in the beauty
Of the sun
Lost to her beau
Lost to her love
Until such time
As always comes
Her heart undone
Came crashing down
Her smile replaced
By a saddened frown
Tears fell down
Her heart ached so
She knew not what
This pain was
How to make it go away
How to continue
To grow through the days

Wanting to die
Tears staining her blue eyes
She wept - her heart so sad
Never knew pain
To hurt so bad
Went to her mother
The sun which
Gave her life
She said not one word
Unto her
She made not one move
Just stood there
Beneath wilting blooms

Blossom of the Sun's Love

Aye the mother
Went to her there
Wrapped her in her arms
Her heart breaking
As her own
Never wishing
Her to know
Such pain could exist
Ahh how she wished
She could take away
The hurt - the pain
To make it her own

Together they cried
For each their own reason
The sun because
Her blossoms heart shattered
Hurt her own
The blossoms heart shattered
Lost to her first love
Together somehow
The found comfort there
Days went by
Tears they cried
Slowly lessoning
The weariness and pain
Allow them both
To regain
Life anew

The daughter of the sun
Blossomed more and more
The mother's grasp
Lessoned with time
But never never
Would they be?
Without the other
To comfort and be
The gentle life
Of the other
Each bringing life
In a different way

The mother sun
Who gave her life
Lived only in the joy
Of her love
Slowly letting her grow
Into womanhood
The blossom who
Without her sun
Could not continue
To grow and become
The most beautiful
Of blossoms
In the garden there
Without her guardian
The protector of her soul
The one who loved her
Enough to let her grow

The Odyssey

A journey traveled
A journey alone
A quest for knowledge
An odyssey to the soul
Forever lingers
Memories of the path
Forever surfaces
A winding road
A journey traversed
A journey forthcoming
A quest for inner peace
An odyssey through time
Reflections of old
Shadows young
Inspiration, Divination
Lessons learned, loves lost
A caravan of thoughts
A carnival of emotions
A longing for serenity
A journey forthcoming
A journey never ending
A quest for knowledge
An odyssey to the soul

Damn! It's Good To Be Back To Me

Shadows dancing across the room
Lost in a memory of you
Wondering how I lived through that hell
I survived it though, some how.
Fights that ended in blood and tears
Fought that fight for so many years
Finally found a way to bring myself back
Give my soul what it lacked
Self respect, self esteem
Damn its good to be back to me

Tears fallen, wiped in vane
Got so tired of it being that way
Hushed of my feelings of my woes
Guessed that was the way love goes
So wrong so very wrong
Almost took a little too long
To get myself back to me
And have the courage to pack and leave.

Here alone and many nights lonely
But its okay because I'm not the only
Woman who had the courage to go
Who left the madness to be alone
Tears falling, let them tumble
This is what makes my soul humble
Through the darkness of this light
I hang on with all my might
Knowing that it won't be long
All the rights that once were wrong
Will one day come to be
Damn its good to be back to me

A Raven Called Out On The Wind

Heart's afire embers burning bright
Garden's abloom under the moon's light
A Raven calls out on the wind
You feel him behind you then
Walking slowly or so it seems
Is he real or just a dream
Eyes piercing your very soul
Wanting to walk away - can't go
Entrapped in his spirit eternally bound
Feel your clothes fall to the ground

Heart's afire embers burning bright
The garden blooms under the pale moonlight
A raven calls out on the wind
Lost to the mortal sins
His hand caresses your pale white face
Leaving a chill with every trace
Staring deep into your eyes
Your modesty to much to hide
A tear wells and falls to your cheek
But words don't come you cannot speak

A Raven Called Out On The Wind

Bodies afire embers dance in delight
Garden moistened under the moonlight
A raven calls out on the wind
He has won your spirit broke you give in
Lips caress your body shudders with touch
Your enjoying this way to much
Slight of hand twist of fate
He runs his fingers across the gardens gate
Heart week soul parched
Below him your body lies arched

Soul's afire embers sparked then ignite
Enters the gardens grove the moonlight
A raven calls out on the wind
Your body rivets as he enters in
The night lit to day
Your body lost along the way
Your name whispered against your skin
As his love comes crashing in
Losing your mind body and soul
Your gardens begin to flow
Blooming there in the moonlight
Embers burning, burning bright
A raven calls out on the wind
As your heart cries out to him

Rapture

I lie there on your bed
Feel the swimming inside my head
Know the pleasures that will come to reside
Deep within this body of mine
Watch as your clothes fall to the floor
Body of iron, hard and strong
Knowing now it won't be long
My mouths' waters warm
Sinfulness comes without warn
Parched by the thirst I've felt so long
Knowing such ecstasy can't be wrong
To taste of you this way
Bring you closer to ecstasy
To the nakedness of me closer I bring you in still
Letting your hands touch me at will
Caresses, kisses showered,
Beneath you my body cowers
Back arching to the pleasure emitting
Moans come forth bodies hitting
Lost to the sea of delight
All walls gone, bodies take flight
Warm waters flow over you now
Can't take the pleasure don't know how
Eyes fall shut as you feel me please
Body shudders with release
Taken you where others fear to go
Taken you inside my womb
Inside your soul is captured
Begging again to feel the rapture.

Lost to the Sadness This Heart Beats Of

Staring in the mirror so long
Reflecting no more, shadows gone
Heart's lost to the journey alone
Not wanting to live on
Here within the catacombs of loves lost
Not able to fill the void fallen to exhaust
Heart beating but living no more
Soul existing but lost to yore

Wishing only for another's touch
Filled with sadness and disgust
Never reaching the rainbows end
Death is what awaits, light dimmed
Darkness shrouding my shadows now
To weak to care, to lost to know how
To find my way back to a world of love
Lost to the sadness my heart beats of

Crying, hurting, holding on
Wondering what went wrong
Wondering what path led me astray
Wishing to be released from this dismay
How is it I came to be so alone
How I am suppose to go on
A heart so strong so true
Blessed not by the love of you

Staring in a mirror so long
Reflecting no more, shadows gone
Beauty lost somewhere within
Never to be touched again
Without the light of your love
Lost to the sadness my heart beats of

Temptations of Imagination

Temptations of Imagination
Reared in dark desires
Unfold beneath the shadows
Of hungers unquenched
Thirst to strong to bear
Reaching for your body
Pangs of lust, animalistic
Instict overcomes
Bodies coupled
In darkened embrace
Burst of colors
Hued by passion
Lovers coiled in unison
Falling to a beat
Of the eternal heart
Imagination of temptation
Exploring the sensations
Set adrift from its spell
Lost to the magic that prevails
Drips of blood
From a golden chalice
Quenches the soul
Bodies unbridled
Filled with desire
Culminating the fire
Temptations of the Imagination

Not Yet

Tired as hell
Sleep won't come
Mind's a jumble
Coming undone
Watchin a sunrise
Tears in my eyes
Can't find solace
Not yet

Pacin the floors
Wishin sleep to come
Drivin me mad
Somethin's gotta be done
Echoing in my head
Can't find rest in this bed
Not yet

Hellish nightmares
Won't leave me be
Close my eyes
Horrid visions - all I see
DAMN wanna sleep just one night
Tired of this frickin fight
Give me sleep or give me death
Not yet

I Called To You

Once so long ago
Back before time
I was adrift there
Lost to a dream
Felt the emotions
Felt the pain
Tears befallen
Heart a calling
Calling for you

Sadness blew
Upon the winds
A raven called
Out for me
I heard and went
Toward the fallen sun
Music played
A melodious tune
Heard myself singing
Singing to you

I called to you
Upon the night
Thought you would come
I sang to you
In my mind
Thought you could hear
My hearts longing
Called out your name
The thunder rang
The birds took flight
I wept
Under the starry night

So there I was
Lost to time
Lost to a longing
Never to be mine
My hearts voice
Never to be heard
My soul's song
Lost to the wind
As I called out
Called out to you again

Tears fallen
Winds calling
Sadness overtaking
Love's heart breaking
I lay my voice to rest
I let the music ravel
Fallen to sleep
One last breath
You name I spoke

Our World Of Immortality

Out into the night
I took my flight
In search of you
As I always do
Scaling the walls
Flying above the trees
Searching for my angel
Who'll keep me alive
Who'll give to me
New found life

Angel, I call to you
Angel, I gotta have you
Need you to come
Follow me
Bring you into
This world
Of Immortality

Can't live this life
Not this long
Not without you
To comfort me
I will die
My soul will starve
Without you
Here to save me

Angel, I call to you
Angel, I gotta have you
Need you to come
Come to me
Bring you into
My world
Of Immortality

I'll shower you
With my love
You'll reign with me
In the heavens above
I'll bring you life
I'll give you eternity
Please, please
Just come to me

Angel, I call to you
Angel, I gotta have you
Need you to come
Come to me
Bring you into
Our world
Of Immortality

Winter's Rain

Quiet settles on the night
The raven calls and then takes flight
I close my eyes imagining you there
Tears fill me from deep within
Your arms do not hold me
Whispers of your voice trail
From nights of yore
When you were there

A neon moon shines high in the sky
Blankets the earth in a shimmer of light
Shadows dance against my heart
You've come to dream with me
Tears fall against my cheek
Dropping to the pillow near
Happiness comes when you are here

A storm comes, the thunder crashed
Against the shores of my soul
A sea of raging sadness
You're to far for me to touch
Reaching out into the shadows of night
I awake to crying out your name
Tears fall like a winters rain

Enraptured

Many dark seasons have come to pass
Since last I seen the light
The midnight forever lingers
Like shadows caressing my soul
Enrapturing me in the bliss of a new dawn
That forever seems too far from reach.
A journey to long to take,
My soul is fragile,
My heart exhausted and lost
To a darkness that sets over me
Casting its eternal shadows of despair
But I linger here in my abyss
In my solemn state of mind
Cradling my darkness
As it devours my very last breath
Sweet surrender of death beckons
Eternal life promised
My last breath becomes my first
Darkness becomes my eternal light
And the seasons of my soul reign on
Enrapturing me in the bliss of a new dawn.

Days of Old

Quiet settles on the night
The raven calls and then takes flight
I close my eyes imagining you there
Tears fill me from deep within
Your arms do not hold me
Whispers of your voice trail
From nights of yore
When you were there

A neon moon shines high in the sky
Blankets the earth in a shimmer of light
Shadows dance against my heart
You've come to dream with me
Tears fall against my cheek
Dropping to the pillow near
Happiness comes when you are here

A storm comes, the thunder crashed
Against the shores of my soul
A sea of raging sadness
You're to far for me to touch
Reaching out into the shadows of night
I awake to crying out your name
Tears fall like a winters rain

Lost To This Hell In Me

All the cobwebs falling about
Darkness where light should be
Lost now to this hell in me
Have to remember
It's all I got
Now that you're gone
My life is lost

Clinging on to what has past
Hoping you will one day come back
To save my empty soul
That once was your home
You lived so deep within
You remain there still
Regret is all that is left

Falling down this wicked well
Feeling it take me deeper still
To the darkness
Lost to the hell in me
Waiting for you to rescue me
Clinging on to what I had
The only thing that keeps me here

Here waiting for you
Here loving you
Here without you
Patiently I wait
Falling deeper still
To the blackness of the cold
That once was warmed by you

Lost to this hell in me
Lost to what was
Lost without you here
Patiently I wait for you
To rescue me from this hell
That has become so commonplace
I wait for you

In The Shadows of a Falling Moon

Morning twilight swallows the moon
The stars above begin to fade
And my lover drifts away
Lost to the night that was our own
Where we danced in the shadows
Of a falling moon

The darkness our blanket
The stars to light our way
As we danced to the music
The heavens angels played
My dress flowing - blowing
In the midnight wind
His smile my heaven
My heart's dance begins
Kept there in the moment
Of true loves delight
He the keeper of
My darkened night
My heart adrift in love
My soul his to own
From the old oak a dove has flown
Beautiful stars falling
Upon the ground below us
We danced there in the shadows
Of a falling moon

His kiss to warm my heart
That once forever cold
His heartbeat the rythm
That lets the dance go on
I feel the magic all around
As we spin - spin and fall
To the dew dropped ground
Tears from a falling moon
Saddened by the sun
Knowing that true love
About to come undone
Will fade unto the shadows
Of a falling moon

Embraced in each's arms
The lovers say goodbye
Tears staining the sadness in their eyes
She weeping under the old oak tree
Losing her true love she so needs
He walking silently into the twilight
As the day returns from night
The music ends, the dance gone
Her heart's woe sings a song
Of a falling moon

Felt You There

Felt you there
So long ago
Knew the love
That burned so deep
An eternal flame
That holds still
Awaiting you
To come back to me

Lost without you
In the corners of my soul
Torn forever
Alone in the shadows
Wishing for you here
Wanting to pull you near
Felt you there
So long ago
Knew the love
I loved to know

Want to cradle you
Protect you from the winds
Hold you close again
Knowing the love
That ages old
Will never die
Felt you there
So long ago
Felt the love
That never dies

A Gypsy Soul

Lost to myself
So far away
Here in the distance
My heart sways
Held here by the magic
Of what is to come
A gypsy soul
Never content to stay
Guess its time
I must be on my way
Come along if you can
Its not that hard
Just take my hand
Together we can go
To places of yore
Where pain and hurt
Are no more
Yes it's true
I must confess
I the gypsy
Who's soul
Never content
Traverses this land
Freedom of heart and soul
Upon a gypsy caravan
Hearts are free
Laughter abounds
Beautiful spirits
All around
This is what I have found
To be my solace
Against the storms
Where pain and sorrows
Are felt no more

A Darkness Reigns

Darkness reigns
These walls my prison
Shackled and chained
To a world which
Has become my own
Since you have gone

Don't know how
How to break free
How to find release
From the darkness
That consumes me

Replaced by the laughter
Is a silence so real
Voices echo in my cell
Walls without pictures
Nights without shadows
I wonder will it ever
Be the same

Don't know how
How to break free
From this prison
That consumes me
A darkness that reigns
Nothing's the same

I sit here betwix these four walls
Pretending its your voice
I hear call
Knowing my imagination
Is playing tricks on me
But its all that I have
To believe in

Don't know how
How to break free
From this prison
From this hell in me
A darkness that reigns
As I slowly go insane

Tears falling upon the sill
A window for watching
For you to return
Only I know this will never be
My crime is loving you
My time eternal
Release won't come for me

Don't know how
How to break free
How to find release
From the darkness
That consumes me

A Spirit With No Place To Go

I watched today as he cried
Holding him close wondering why
Wondering how to take away
The sadness in his soul this day
A beautiful man, his eyes bright
Filled with passion filled with might
Shadowed by a pain
Knowing him to change
Shattered heart, torn soul
A spirit without a place to go

Aching from so deep inside
Hurt by the tramas that reside
Within his heart that I cannot save
For the spirit so enslaved
Wanting only to return his smile
To walk with him across the miles
To be the gentle rocking of his sea
To return the love that used to be
Wound so deep within his soul
Captured by a spirit's glow

Comforting arms hold him close
Just what he needed most
A shelter from the storms within
A way to hold on to what one can
Without losing site of now
For learning to go on, knowing how
This I cannot give to him
He so lost within
The shadows of true hearts woe
A spirit with no place to go

A Long Day's Pains

So many nights
I dreamed you were there
Holding me close
Feeling you care
Taking away my woes
From a long days pains

Being my comfort
Behind the scenes
You the rescue
My port in the storm
You the lover
Who heals my soul
To take away my woes
From a long days pains

Will I ever find you there
A shadow no more
The realness of your body
The wholeness of you soul
Lying beside me
When the nights are cold
Telling me you care
When its my body you hold

Closing my eyes
I try and find sleep
My heart adrift, my soul weeps
You're not here
Not just yet
But one day
I will awaken to find
My dream come true
You beside me
To take away my woes
And the pains of a long day
Will matter no more

Needing You

You can't hear
The screams inside me
You can't see
The torment
That surrounds me
Diving under
Into a world of you
Lost in the presence
Of something lost to me
Not knowing which way to turn
Feeling lost without you
Broken down and beaten
Can't fight anymore
Heart's lost to the depths
Of the tears in me
Needing you
Needing me
Wanting you
So deep in me
Fighting a ghost
That won't go away
Haunting me
Hurting me
Needing you
Needing me

The Storm

As I stood upon the shore
Watching the gray clouds drift in
I called to my true love
Lost against the wind
So far out in the raging sea
Would he ever come back to me

North winds blowing
Down across the bay
The night would be cold
And my heart so alone
Without him here
I am not whole

Thunders roared in silent night
The moon veiled by dark clouds
The storm is coming to shore
The wall between him and I
Hopes that dawn will bring
My true love back to me

A messenger comes to call
Running fast against the knoll
My heart sinks, an ache creeps into my soul
Face flushed and eyes sad
He tells me what I did not want to hear
My true loves ship will not come to shore

To my knees I fell
Clutching his shirt
Screaming out his name
Tears lost in vain
What God of the Sea
Could take my true love from me

As I stood upon the shore
Watching the gray clouds drift in
I called to my true love
Lost against the wind
So far out in the raging sea
Never to come back to me

Touching You

Feeling you
Next to me
My heaven
Touching you
Bodies as one
My abyss
Your heartbeat
Resounding in me
Becoming my life
Becoming me
Loving you
Hurting inside
Wanting always
To feel you
Next to me
Touching you
Bodies as one
Feel your heartbeat
Alive in me
Lost to my heaven
Living in your soul
No longer cold
Alive in you
Alive in me
Death forsaken
Dreams reality
Feeling you
Next to me
Touching me
The way

I Die

As your love embraces me
Taking each breath from me
Don't know how to stop
That which takes over
Don't want to stop
Drowning in you
Swallowing me in
I die
For you

My soul lost to the abyss
My heart filled with song
But pain and sadness still
Can't keep going down
Can't hold my breath any longer
Drowning in you
Swallowing me in
I die
Without you

So far away yet so near
Things so unclear
Can't find you anywhere
Can't live without you there
Want to die in the love
That once was ours
Drowning in you
Swallowing me in
I die
Waiting for you

Wanting it to be a dream
Wanting my dreams to come true
Wanting to die in this love for you
Can't find you anywhere
Can't live without you there
Without you living in my soul
The world grows forever cold
Drowning in you
Swallowing me in
So alone
I die
Without you

Scream At Me

Can't you say what's on your mind
Scream at me
Do anything
Just don't kill me with the silence
Gotta know what's in your heart
Before I fall completely apart
You're my everything
Lost forever to an aching
That just won't go away
Needing you to complete my soul
Darkness lives without you
So alone in the terrible hell
That has become my life without you
Gotta say something now
Can't let this go on
Can't go on without knowing
Scream at me
Do anything
The silence is killing me
Breaking my heart to a million pieces
Needing you
Wanting you
Losing you
Can't bear the pain
Gotta get away
Needin' to run back to you
Back to the center of my soul
Forever ours if you just say so
Gotta talk to me
Gotta tell me how
To make it without you
Scream at me
Say anything
Just don't let this silence
Bury me

ೞ

An Angel

I have fallen
To the wonders
Of an angel
Who's heart
So pure
Does not know
Of his beauty.

He does not see
How his soul emits
A happiness
In the face of sadness
How his aura
Has affected me.

I have fallen
To the beauty
Of an angel
Who knows not
How I see
More than the
Naked eye reveals.

His voice a melody
An embodiment of art
Beautiful colors
On the page of a song
He does not know
How he moves me.

So happy
Yet so saddened
His beauty
Untold
His spirit
A vision
To behold.

A soul strong
Lost to a body so weak
Unable to hide
Who he truly is
An angel fallen
Unto me.

A Lullaby

A melody plays
Inside my head
A lullaby
To soothe
My hearts tears
It echoes
So deep within
I am drifting
Away from
The pain
Angels dancing
All about
Rock me gently
To ease
My sadness
To take away
The long days
Without you

A lullaby
To help me
Move on
To help me
Find peace
Through my nights
Because the days
Are so filled
With tears
With sadness
And pain
A melody plays
Inside my head
Angels rock
My heart to rest
A lullaby
To soothe
My hearts fears
Fears of never
Seeing you again
Of never holding
You close
To help me find
A way
To let go
To find peace
So that I
May find
Quiet sleep

The Loneliness of My Soul

I close my eyes
In hopes of finding you there
The angel that lifts me from this fall
So spiraling, so blinding
I know you exist
If only in my dark abyss

Wising upon a fallen star
Grabbing hold of its tails
As it soars from the heavens above
Just as I go falling down
Tumbling, Crying
As it falls
Through the darkness of my soul.

None to comfort me
None to enwrap me in their love
So the journey I take alone
Gathering a touch here and there
Stumbling, Staggering
Feeding upon what moments are given
Letting it feed my hunger
Never to be relinquished

So as I pass slowly by
Through my world alone
There is but nothing
So sad as the loneliness of my soul
The angel has left me to fall
Downward, Falling
My soul weeps but for you
The angel that will take me away
From this darkened state
That has become my existence

So lost, so alone

Eternal Damnation

Desolation and Despise
All that surrounds me now
So lost to the world of darkness
Forever my eternal damnation
Cut by a knife
Never to bleed
For all the blood runs cold in me
Wishing only to fall away from this eternal night
To find my way back up
From whence I began to fall
Seeing all others surround me
In clouds of light and smiles
Finding I am unable to speak
My muse but drawn to darkness
To bleed To bleed
How can I ever return
From the eternal night
That has become my damnation
The aura that surrounds me now
So ebony with blood stained tears
All that is reminisant of the blood
That once was warm within me
Taken from the world of others
To suffer here in my solitude
That has become my eternal damnation

Sweet Imaginations

Lost in a dream
An imagination of you and me
Alone in the quiet of the night
Together there in the candlelight
Music is playing soft and soothing
Its your heart I am holding
Wrapped there in the moment
Lost to ourselves
In a moment of love
Giggles among us
Talking light and low
I take your hand
Into a dance we go
Holding each other
Nothing matters
Just the fact that we're together
This is my dream
My dream for you and me
A quiet evening
Where two hearts sing
Where love lights the room
All our thoughts carried
From one to the other
Where each is all we need
This is my dream of you and me
A sweet imagination
That carries me through the day
Knowing by your side I will be coming
Home to stay

My Nirvana

Smoke hazed room
A reflection of my doom
Entered in without a care
Knowing my drug would be there
Had to have the remedy
That would eventually kill me

To the back room I go
Didn't care, didn't know
What would happen this time
As I shot the poison inside
Laid back on a couch

Ready for my medicine
Body shaking, mind breaking
Feel the coolness through my veins
Feel the lessoning of the pain
Overcome in my nirvana
No more will, no more drama
Dreams take me far away

Feel the shaking, hear the cries
As they try to awaken me
Only this time I want to sleep
Don't wanna come back down again
Don't wanna let them in

Body lifting watching over
The scene below me as I wonder
Only to come to the realization
That this time my salvation
Was my death

The Angel of Death

The Angel of Death
Beckons to me
Calling me to his bed
Where my soul shall rest
Tempting me with fruits
Of the dead
I'll follow him when he comes
Down his sinful road
To which there is no end
Seeing my sadness
He comes to call
To play upon the woes
Of a soul fallen
Enchanting me
With beauty and life
Telling me everything
Will be alright
Touching me
In all the right places
The masquerade
Of many faces
I'll succumb to his trance
As I fall to dance
There in the bed
Of the Angel of Death
Who has come for me

Mad Woman In The Graveyard Growing Old

Walking through the rain today
Felt the sadness felt the pain
As I walked closer still
Didn't know if I had the will
To the place you lay in eternal rest
Heart and soul put to the test
Can I live without you now
Don't know how
Don't know how

Anger boils under my skin
Haven't felt so mad since God knows when
Pissed for having to let you go
Sad and crying feelin so low
Watched as your bed was lowered in
Wondering if you were within
Or floating about in the shadows above
Losing my senses lost my love

Dirt covered your new home
Feeling like I'm so alone
Need you to come back to me
Lost to the darkness of the seas
Storms brewing overhead
Wishing now I too was dead
Screaming out for you to hear
Trying to keep you forever near
Won't let go of the memories of you
Can't forget you.

Such a vision for others to behold
A mad woman in the graveyard growing old
Dying slowly from a broken heart
Heart dying falling apart
Her true love today laid in the ground
Feeling her world spinning around
Dizzied by the pains of loss
Heartache so rich can't pay the cost
To feel the pain taken away
As she laid her true love down today

Two Lovers Dance

Two souls dancing upon the night
Lost to a love two hearts delight
Skies of gray under a neon moon
Knowing this time will end soon
Lovers lost to these moments in time
Dance beneath the long raging vines
Enwrapping them together as one
A love too true to come undone

Her dress of white floating adrift
Lost to the moments in his kiss
Bodies descend to the ground below
Letting their hearts unfold
Opening unto the other with ease
Hearts afloat upon open seas
Creatures of the night stand by
Lost to the beauty before their eyes

Two souls entrapped in one
A love to strong to be undone
Magically dancing upon the night
Under the spell of the moon's light
Night descends upon the land
Embraced, entwined, hand in hand
The lovers take a journey to the soul
Never to return further they go
Down the path of eternal night
Two lovers dance beneath the moonlight

So Tired of Being Here

I'm so tired of being here
Washed away in all my tears
Feelin like the scars will never heal
The pain too strong too real
Wishin it would all just go away
Captivated by wounds of yesterday
Struggling to find all that was lost
Knowing it to be not worth the cost

All the time does not heal
That which my heart did feel
Now so numb so cold
Abandoned to the world alone
I kept a vigil for you deep within
Awaiting when you would return again
To save me from the dark abyss
To come walking through the mourning mists

You come not unto me
To save me from the swallowing seas
That have engulfed my heart and soul
Lost for an eternity now alone
God can't you hear my cries!?!
Why don't you come, why!?!
To feel once more your warm embrace
Would take away the chill so commonplace
Embers long lost to ash and dust
Lost angry and without trust
Washed away in all these tears
I'm just so tired of being here.

Building Anticipation

I look into your eyes
I see the desire burning there
Wanting me, needing me
Your eyes a glow with passion
I savor this moment
Yearning for your touch
Wavering in the moment
To build anticipation

A game of lovers choice
A conscious awareness of
What sensuality awaits
When the moment comes
I make you wait

You know my darkest secrets
You feel my heart's desire
You take this to the brink
Of a lost return
Leaving me wanting you
Needing you more
To build anticipation

A dance of the divine
A melody of delight
Fills me, warms the chill
Fascinated from the thrill
You make me wait

Staring back at you
Undressing you with my eyes
Taking in the largeness of your size
Mouth watering, soul yearning
To feel the touch of your hands
Against my skin
Anticipation weakens me

଼

Caressing my face
While your fingers trace
An outline of my body
Deep within your mind
Envisioning the warmth
That awaits and beckons
Calling to you in a whisper
Anticipation weakens you

Building anticipation
Weakening our discretion
Wanting needing the others love
Befallen to our thoughts
Adrift in a sea of lust
Wanting Needing
Fallin to touch

Building anticipation
Overtaken
I touch your skin
You touch mine
Lips caress
Bodies divine
Nakedness prevails
Our bodies unveiled

Frozen, bodies chilled
The touch to much a thrill
Ecstasy flows
Bodies enfold
You take me deeper
I welcome you to enter
As you begin again
To build anticipation

Days In The Shadows

Days in the shadows
One day just like the rest
Found a spot to lay my weary head
Lost to a world far from the others
My world of hunger
The never-ending pain
Caused my life
To Fall away

Wandering one place to the other
Storms blinding my eyes
The cold winters wind chilled me
To the edges of my soul
Lost to memories of a day forever gone
Wondering would I ever make it home

Lying awake under a midnight sun
Felt the urge to come undone
Arms uplifting me to another realm
Took away my hunger
Fed my sorrows
Found my way back
Seeing my tomorrows
Cries no longer echoing
From the depths of my heart

Voices

Jesus can you hear their cries
Cover my ears - close my eyes
The voices never stop calling
Into this pit I just keep falling
Lost to the voices in my head
Wishin I could just go to bed
To fall away to silent sleep
Where the voices do not seek
To torture my mind and soul
Where the voices cannot go
Drivin me crazy - drivin me mad
If you only knew how bad
Jesus can you hear their cries
I'm dying from the inside
Can't get them out of my head
Can't find sleep in my bed
Death is the only way
To keep the voices at bay
I don't wanna die
I don't wanna cry
I just want them to go away
Jesus can you hear their cries
I get a blade out of the drawer
Stand there staring at the floor
Watching the blood pooling around
Watching the voices fall to the ground
Jesus can you hear their cries
No I can't, not this time

Still of Night

I lie here in the still of night
Filled with sadness filled with fright
Scared of what the morrow will bring
Scared that my heart will never sing
Of true love that seems never my own
Scared that I will forever be alone
My heart scarred my soul sore
My soul breathes no more

I take a breath trying to find life
Somewhere here in the still of night
Reaching across this lonely bed
My worst fear my dread
Greets me with the emptiness I find
Losing my will, losing time
To repair the heart that beats no more
My heart scarred, my soul sore

Missing an angel who never comes
Feeling my soul come undone
Calling to him in the still of this night
Tears falling, losing sight
Of a dream that once was my own
My hearts to weak to go on
I fall to the pillow wet with tears
To frightened to face my fears
My heart scarred, my soul sore
My soul breaths no more

I lie here in the still of night
Filled with fear, filled with fright
The tears will never stop falling
My heart never stops calling
Hoping that the morrow will bring
The angel who will make my heart sing
The man whose love will be my own
The love that will help me live on
Without this loneliness in my soul

Have You Seen His Beauty?

How would you
describe a man
whose beauty
is beyond awe

How would you capture
a soul so free
This you know
Can never be
A gift to hold
Within your heart

You want so badly
To be a part
of the beauty that lives
Deep within his spirit
Too far from your reach

Beauty that makes
Your soul's heart weep
Longing so painful
True love so deep
How could you compare

How could you return
The feelings emitted
How could you comfort
A soul like his
So angelic and pure

Have you seen this angel
Did you feel his awe
Did you fall in love
With a heart so true
How did you go on

A spirit a glow
A soul in flight
A love you long for
On the passing
Of your heart's dreams

Captured by none
He's gone again
Sadness in your heart
Fills you till you're mad
Have you seen his beauty
As I have

This Cold In Me

Fallen embers
Burning bright
Lost to the beauty
Of the night
The oceans breeze
So warm and free
Flows across
The open seas
Alone I sat
Upon the shore
Lost to a thought
Of times ago
Of times no more
Times when I knew
What it was
To know the joy
To know the love
So alone so far away
From the joys
Of yesterday
Fallen embers
Burning bright
Wishing you
Were here tonight
The ocean's breeze
So warm and free
Doesn't take away
This cold in me

Reflection

Looking into the mirror
My mirror of truth
The one that reflects
My inner self
I see the person
You see everyday
But the reflection
So different
Do you know me?
How could you?
I don't even know myself
This image that projects
A soul captured
In a body of lies
A smile not my own
A heart filled with sadness
Eyes that project
The images of myself
Falling behind the shadows
Which have become
The person you now see
The one I cannot find
The one who reflects
For the world to see
But cannot disguise
As she reflects upon my eyes
Who is she?
How does she live?
Knowing of her inner sins
To be the one
You wish her to be
To reflect a soul
That doesn't belong to her
A soul filled with lies
As she sees
Her true reflection
In her mirror of shadows
Cast down on her

Rest In Peace

Rest in peace
I heard him calling
As the crowd departed
Tears stained his blue eyes
Saddened as they entered
My body in the ground

Handfuls of dirt thrown down
Roses now my blanket
Coldness gathering around me
Darkness covering the sun
Rest in peace
I heard a teardrop falling

Lying there just listening
To the sounds of death
I heard footsteps
Coming back
Soft upon the ground
Heard a whisper of a sound

Rest in peace
I heard him crying
Knowing that inside
He was dying
Wanting so bad
To wrap my arms around him
Hold him close again

Laid his head down
To the ground
Asking can you hear me now
My heart still beats of you
Don't know what I will do
Rest in peace
I heard him whisper

Screaming from the Inside
Trying to make my voice heard
Didn't know how
To reach him now
Tears falling
As I heard his voice calling
Rest in Peace

Can't Help I'm Not The Same

Just because I haven't the time
Doesn't mean you're not on my mind
Can't help this spirit in me
Always drifting wanting to be free
Warm sunsets calling my name
Can't help I'm not the same
Same as all the others
Same as the usual lover
When I'm with you again
You feel the love deep within
Our bodies gently adrift
Lost to the fog, lost to the mist
Feel the soul of a gypsy
Come along - come with me
Lets see the morning sun rise
Walk here by my side
Feel my spirit unveil
Know this as love, not your hell
And when I drift away
Know I'm not gone to stay
I'll be back again soon
Maybe some warm afternoon
While your laying in a field of green
Lost to yourself in a wondrous dream
There, there, is where I will be.

Eyes of Ecstasy

Passionate kisses
Warm embrace
Lips caressing
Eyes fall back
Swept in desire
Body trembles
At your touch
Wanting needing
Hunger prevails
Cradled against you
Bodies touching
Fires burning
Wetness rains
Waters rushing
Eyes open
Visions appear
Dancing bodies
Erotic collision
Sensual emotions
Delightful bliss
Immortal ecstasy
Beautiful kiss
Eyes close
Bodies waver
Rest comes
Dreams savor

A Canvas of White

He sits down
To a canvas of white
His mind drifts off
To find peace within
His hands begin to paint
The images in his mind
That never stop coming
From the corners of his soul
Beauty drawn out
Fingers of gold
Raging emotions flow
From my eyes I see art formed
As he sketches out images
We can only hold
Deep within the shadows
Never to be told
His story comes to life
As he sits down
To a canvas of white

Fallen Sunsets

As the sun rises over the land
I imagine there I hold your hand
I walk with you in the morning mists
Lost to a conversation that doesn't exist
I feel your love protecting me
Lost to a moment of beauty

As the sun sets over the land
I lie in bed and feel your hand
Touching me so deep within
Holding me close again
Lost to a dream so far from me
Lost to what I wished could be

Morning sun rises in the sky
Lost to visions of wishful lies
Sun setting, darkness draws near
Holding on wishing you here
Reality fallen to dreams
Lost my mind or so it seems
Conversations that don't exist
Love lost in the mists
Of days and nights gone by
Fallen sunsets and morning sun rise

You Can Never Go

You see me
Across a crowded room
Drawn by my essence
Pulled closer to my charms
You come
As I wished you would

Eyes of the deepest blue
Eyes that lure you
Deeper into my darkness
From which you have no release
Calling to you from the deep
You feel my spirit, touch my soul
For now you can never let go

The capture of your senses
The depth of my perceptions
Bringing you deeper into my world
Feel your body begin to whirl
Down into the exotic, darkened abyss
Surrendering to its essence

Tis the magic of which you were warned
Now your soul forever torn
Unable to find escape from me
Never wanting to be released
Drunken by my desire
Burning in my fires
The phantom of your thoughts
Its too late now
You're soul's been sought

Close your eyes begin to fall
All your powers dissolved
Lost to the essence
Of my presence
I the darkness you adore
I the reason you are lured
Deeper into the darkness you go
Lost to what you do not know
All you perceive lost in me
All you desire aflame in my fire

I now the darkness you crave
I the only that can save
Your soul from its yearning
Your heart from its burning
The addiction that drunkens you so
The reason you can never let go

Whispers of The Soul Emit

Pulled the blinds, candles burn bright
Smokey glaze through the yellow light
Looked at you with starry eyes
Pulled you closer by my side
Watching me watching you
Lost to a sea of blue
Lips come close to a touch
Hinting of what's to come
Hands find their way
To reach the heart of the other
Whispers of the soul emit

Dazed by the energy
That begins to flow
Lost to the feelin
Not wanting to let go
Bodies undress
Skin touches skin
With warm embrace
Breath becomes shallow
As the two lovers swim
In a sea of desires
Drowning in each other

Whispers of the soul emit
Touched by your embrace
Words unspoken
Not needing to be said
Felt to the depths
Drawn from the heart
This moment eternal
Even when bodies part

Desires and Lust
Taken hold and overtook
Two lovers in the shadows of their day
Fallen to the loneliness of each ones soul
Driven to each other like stormy winds
Now lay resting from the night they spent
Lost in a world of tumbles and love
Can't go back to the way it was
Whispers of the soul emit

The Forest

A dark forest
Over the dale
Lies in wait
For those who believe
That magic lies within
It's grove of trees.

The trees sway
From side to side
Greeting you
As you go by
Inviting you
To come on through
To find your way
Down their lonely paths
That never seem to end
But always take you
Where you've never been.

Wanting to blanket you
In a sea of green
Strength and wisdom
Yet to be seen
Oh how they long
For someone to
Notice their song
Breezes flowing
In and out
How could you not go
Through the forest
Into the grove

Two Lost Souls

Two lost souls adrift in the night
Hearts saddened by the pains of life
She saw him across a crowded room
He saw her eyes so blue
He watched her lost in thought
She lowered her eyes a tear dropped
The sadness that shown
Replaced his own

He walked over asking if she would
She took his hand as she stood
They fell to the darkened floor
Feeling a lightness where before
Only sadness lay at their doors
She felt his arms holding her tight
He held her close in the dimmed light
Their two lost souls found each other
In the arms of one another

Dancing, swaying to the sounds
Forgetting all that did surround
They were one without a care
He buried his head in her hair
She felt her heart begin to rush
Finger to mouth he whispered hush
He kissed her lips so soft and sweet
Uplifting her soul off its feet

Twirling around in sadness there
He took away all her cares
They danced until the night was through
But to leave the other neither could do
He walked her home
Along the cobblestones
And just as she was about to go in
He ask when he could see her again

ൣ

Two Lost Souls

Her heart uplifted eyes beaming bright
Said please don't leave me tonight
He kissed her hard upon her lips
Putting his hand around her hips
Two lost souls under the eave
By the porch under the tree
Two lost souls adrift in flight
Found each other under the pale moonlight

She took his hand and led him in
Her thoughts consuming her of her sins
But too sad to care,
She needed him there
To take away all the lonely nights
That had become her life
She kissed his lips so much passion inside
She lay down upon her bed he by her side

They made love the night through
Tumbling and loving as true lovers do
Not even knowing the other so much
Lost to the wonders of each's touch
Shadowing the sadness if for a moment in time
Lost in the pleasures, they crossed a line
Followed a lovers heart of desire
Burning embers of a dying fire

Two lost souls adrift in the pains of life
Hearts comforted upon this night
Will rise as the morning comes
Knowing what's done is done

☙

Two Lost Souls

He wakes in her arms there
Losing his soul feeling despair
She reaches over holding on
Knowing if he leaves their moment gone
Tears falling upon her cheek
Feeling her heart growing weak
His eyes filled and on the ridge
Realizing what he did
Kissed her softly catching her tears
Trying to hide his own fears

She held his hand and pulled him near
Holding him close she whispered in his ear
Please don't leave me not so soon
The fell to sleep till afternoon
Both dreading what was to come
Afraid again to be numb
He held her close again that night
Making love to her with all his might

He never did get up and leave
Because in his heart he believed
She the angel come to save his soul
She the one who made him whole
She stayed with him through the years
Through the laughter, happiness and tears
Two lost souls came to be
A dance of lovers through eternity

The Ghosts' Tale

Did you see a ghost tonight?
He ask his love.
Aye my love I did,
Only one.
A shadow in the mist of time
Beheld by my eyes,
Lost to the others, he drifted by.
Wandering the soul's lost path
Wavering in the winds of age,
Searching for his true love
Lost to him in death.

How did he lose his love?
He asked in sadness for this soul.

The tale is of sorrow, my lord,
She was but a young lass,
Full of life.
Soon to be wed,
Soon to be his wife.
So much in love he gave
His heart unto her.
Wept from her beauty,
Filled with the happiness,
Only true love possesses.

She was but out a walking
Upon the grassy knoll,
When a band of warriors
Came through their grove.
They took their prize in her,
And thus she died.

He wept he cried
To no avail to no return
Wishing he could be with her
Missing the scent of her hair
The smile that made him whole
Without her his spirit cold
Dying inside from the pain
He called to her upon the nigh
With tears in his eyes

When answer did not come
He knew nothing left to be done
He hung himself in the great oak
In order to join her there
Lost to his heart's sorrow
Lost to her death
He walked the path
That would lead him back
To his true love
Who lived now with the angels above

His heart hung heavy,
Understanding not
He ask his love how he got lost...

The Ghosts' Tale

Aye my lord, it is but sad
He has searched all the land
Lost to the sands of time
He searches on without fail
Calling to her upon the nigh
He weeps and cries
For only to find his true love
Would bring his heart such joy
But to no avail, to no return
She is but gone lost forever
To the mist of time
Wandering the soul's lost path
Wavering in the winds of age
Searching for her true love
Lost to her in death

The two lovers lost to thought
Reached for the other
Sadden from the ghosts' tale
Sorrowed by his loss
Praying they would never face
Such an agony of the heart
As the two lovers who
Roam about the knoll
Reaching for their true love
Never to be found

Tears held back
He kissed her then
Promising his true love
He would meet her there
There at the great oak tree
Should such ever a fate come to be
For he could not bear the thought
That their two hearts ever be lost
From each other as these souls

She wept in happiness
As his promise was given
She too avowed never
To leave the great oak until
Such time as he could come
To hold her close again

They lay back upon the knoll
Watched as the mist settled
Across the moon
Forever in love they knew
Never would they be
a ghost wandering the soul's lost path
Wavering in the winds of age
Searching for their true love
Lost to them in death

Left Behind

Got so much on my mind
It's tearing at my insides
Wishin for something just can't have
Feelin like life's gone bad
Wondering why I get up each day
Knowing that nothin will change
Somewhere got left behind
Time's no longer on my side
See hopes and dreams fading to black
Strugglin to just get back
Back to a place where it's alright
Out of the darkness that has become my life
Growing old in this heart of mine
Knowing I'm running out of time
Will those dreams all fade to dust
Can't have faith can't trust
Left behind here all alone
Just can't feel there's any hope

Dawn Fades To Night

Just as the dawn fades to night
I close my eyes close them tight
Watch as the world falls away
Feel the pain of yesterdays
Wonder will I ever get back again
To the way I was back then
Wonder if I can have the life of days gone
Wonder what I did wrong
Searching for a better tomorrow
Trying to wash away these sorrows
Hangin by a frayed piece of string
Knowing that tomorrow won't bring
Back the fullness of a life once mine
Want to turn back time
Start all over again
Just don't know where to begin
So just as dawn fades to night
I close my eyes close them tight
Feel as the tears fall away
Knowing tomorrow will be like yesterday

Befallen

Befallen to a moment to much to bear
Longings dwell lost my will to care
Let you into my secret world
Your touch so gentle so warm
To a cold and lonely soul
Felt my body letting go
Your breath so close so near
Vision blurred all unclear
Passion unfolding in your kiss
Filling me with moments missed
Eyes inviting me closer still
Lost my spirit broke my will
Befallen to a moment in time
Lost to the comfort of your hand in mine
Soul burning for your touch
Heart falling, it was too much
To bear the pain that was going away
The beauty that it portrayed
Out of darkness into light
Befallen to the spell of night
Bodies touching passion flowing
Felt my will as it was going
Away into the darkness free to see light
Of a moment that restored life
To a soul lost to darkness and cold
A soul that was growing old
From the lack of human touch
Befallen to a moment
Because I needed you so much
To give life to a heart that beats no more

A Blanket For Scars

Inside thy heart,
A darkness falls,
Blanketing the scars
That are pained with sadness
Wounds that ache
And are deeper than great seas
There was a great battle
That took no sympathy
It took what lay innocent
Then turned it to pain
Eyes wide open
New life within
Stolen like a baby
From its crib.
No mercy shown
Beautiful happiness
Taken away
No regard for what would come
When darkness fell upon this soul

My Time To Fly

A door was opened
So I left
Out into the sunset
Where I was meant to be
Caged in a life
That was not my own
A life that left me
With a soul torn

Into the darkness
I found my way
Under a firey moon
That became my guide
Didn't know where
Didn't know why
Just knew it to be
My time to fly

Letting Go

Letting go is so hard to do
Finding the strength
To do what's right
Knowing from the depths within
That your heart longs
To soar upon the wind
Having the courage
To let go
Are we meant
To follow the rest
Was it intended
For us to be our best
Should we feel the guilt
Of following our hearts
Should we embrace
The chance to make a new start

Let your spirit go
Feel the love begin to flow
Illuminating the depths of your heart
The shadows of your soul
Could it be so wrong
To want this for ourselves
Are we suppose to place
Our desires and dreams
Upon the shelf
If it feels to scary
To do on your own
Just take my hand
I won't leave you alone
I have the same hopes
And needs as you
And believe it or not
I'm scared too
But together perchance
What one heart
Cannot attain
Together
Two will find a way

Long Lost Mind

Sittin here
Can't find sleep
Mind's a blank
Soul's at peace
Body quenched
No longer aches
Wondering
What is this place
Haven't been here
In quite sometime
A state
Of a long lost mind

Been so long
Since I felt
My mind at ease
To exist yet
Feel pleased
Peace so afar
Didn't realize
I was struggling so hard
Just trying to get back
Trying to return
Haven't been here
In such a long time
A state
Of a long lost mind

A tranquil shroud
Enrobes me now
Blankets away
A lost feeling
Of pain
A soul longing
Just trying to find
A state
Of my long lost mind

Have come
To the conclusion
It wasn't just
A wishful delusion
I've been here before
Lest I couldn't
Yearn for return
To the calm
Here among my storm
A harmony of mind
And Soul
A state
Of reunion
A return
Of my long lost mind

A Piano Plays Softly

A piano plays softly
Somewhere in the back of my mind
Lost to its melody
That unfolds the corners of thought
Memories come to light
Happiness fades to black
Drifting in and out of this reality
That somehow became my life
Searching for answers I'll never find
Waiting for the dawn of my time
A day when unraveled becomes whole
Sorrows fall to the wayside
And a piano plays softly
From the shadows of my soul

Eyes Closed

Eyes closed
Darkness my veil
Echoes of your voice I hear
Whispers bring us oh so near
Shadows of our bodies intertwined
Dreams of ecstasy, dreams divine
Soft gentle touches, warm embrace
The outline of your face my fingers trace
Each night as darkness prevails
I'll seek you on this long winding trail
Wandering alone here you're so far away
Eyes closed
Your here to stay

Lover's Drum

As I embrace your head gently
Within my breast
Hear my heart beating gently
Like the evening sun sets
Sweetly the rythm
Of a lover's drum beats
As our souls drift together
And softly retreat
To a world of great visions
Where lovers do meet
Where words are not spoken
And softly softly
The lover's drum beats

Here With You

Although I am no longer here
Please know I am forever near
I walk with you in sadness
I stand beside you in pain
My heart breaks each time
You cry out my name
I didn't mean to go
I always wanted to stay
This I hope you know
Every time your heart beats
I feel it deep within my soul
Every breath you take
Becomes my own
I live through you
Through your love
That which gives me life
So that I may forever be
Here with you